To:

From:

Published in the United States by Random House Children's Books,
a division of Penguin Random House LLC, New York.
The artwork that appears herein was adapted from the book *Go, Dog. Go!*,
copyright © 1961 by P. D. Eastman, and copyright renewed 1989 by Mary L. Eastman.

Random House and the colophon are registered trademarks of Penguin Random House LLC.

Visit us on the Web!
rhcbooks.com

Educators and librarians, for a variety of teaching tools, visit us at
RHTeachersLibrarians.com

ISBN 978-0-593-18121-8

MANUFACTURED IN CHINA   10 9 8 7 6 5 4 3 2 1   First Edition

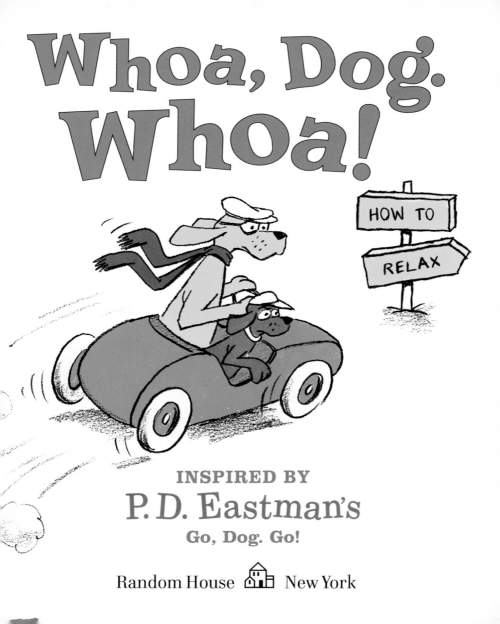

Whoa, Dog. Whoa!

HOW TO

RELAX

INSPIRED BY

P. D. Eastman's

Go, Dog. Go!

Random House 🏠 New York

Are you always **racing** from place to place?

Does it seem like nothing ever goes **right**?

You need to **STOP**!

Learn to enjoy
simple pleasures!

Take a **walk**.
Get some fresh air.

Play a **game**.
Play **music**.

Put your feet up.

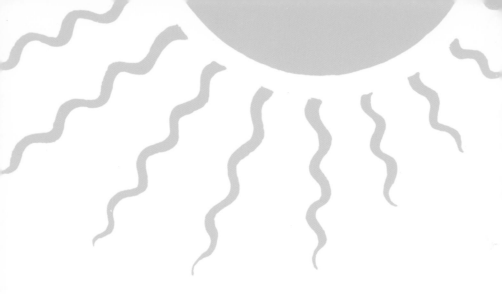

Relax a little.

Read a good book.

Do something
just for the
fun of it.

Hang out
with your
friends.

Because life is a party, and you only get **one** invitation.

So take a break.
You deserve it!

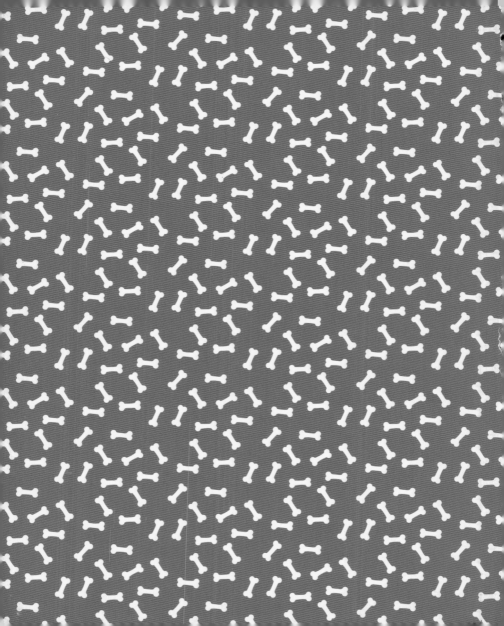